GROVER
CLEVELAND

PRESIDENTIAL ✦ LEADERS

GROVER CLEVELAND

RITA J. MARKEL

TWENTY-FIRST CENTURY BOOKS/MINNEAPOLIS

To Bill & Bernice

Twenty-First Century Books
A division of Lerner Publishing Group
241 First Avenue North
Minneapolis, MN 55401 U.S.A.

Website address: www.lernerbooks.com

Library of Congress Cataloging-in-Publication Data

Markel, Rita J.
    Grover Cleveland / by Rita J. Markel.
        p.   cm. — (Presidential leaders)
    Includes bibliographical references (p.) and index.
    ISBN-13: 978-0-8225-1494-7 (lib.bdg. : alk. paper)
        ISBN-10: 0-8225-1494-X (lib. bdg. : alk. paper)
        1. Cleveland, Grover, 1837–1908—Juvenile literature. 2. Presidents—United States—
Biography—Juvenile literature. I. Title. II. Series.
    E697 .M37 2007
    973.8'5092—dc22   2005032493

Manufactured in the United States of America
1 2 3 4 5 6 – JR – 12 11 10 09 08 07

CONTENTS

———— ✧ ————

At the Erie County, New York, gallows (above), Sheriff Cleveland, a future U.S. president, personally served as executioner.

INTRODUCTION

*Let me rise or fall, I am going to work for the
interests of the people.*
—Grover Cleveland, speech given in August 1882

Patrick Morrissey was going to be executed by public hanging
in Erie County, New York, on September 6, 1872. His crime?
He had stabbed his own mother to death in an argument over
money. As expected, a crowd gathered to watch the hanging.
But the spectators were disappointed. They found the gallows
surrounded by screens that blocked their view. The new county sheriff, Grover Cleveland, had put the screens up for the
day. Cleveland did not believe it was right for the public to
watch this event. Morrissey was hanged in private.

Although Cleveland did not oppose the death sentence, the
idea of ending another person's life disturbed him. Unlike
other sheriffs, he did not hire someone else to do the job.
How could he ask someone else to do what he did not want
to do himself? Cleveland climbed the steps of the gallows that
September morning, reached out his hand, and released the
trapdoor.

This sense of duty and honor made people respect and trust Cleveland as a public official. He rose quickly in politics. He went from serving as mayor of Buffalo, New York, to president of the United States in just three years. In a time of widespread dishonesty in public office, he stood out as someone who held fast to his values. The *New York World* newspaper, which was owned by the famous publisher Joseph Pulitzer, gave four reasons to back Cleveland: "He is honest. He is honest. He is honest. He is honest."

When Cleveland told a friend that he was going to work for the people's interests, he meant what he said. During his two terms as president, Cleveland defended what he saw as those interests. At various times, war veterans, farmers, and politicians of both parties were angry with him. That did not stop Cleveland. He did what he thought was right anyway.

CHAPTER ONE

A GOOD FOUNDATION

George Washington improved his time when he was a boy and he was not sorry.

—Stephen Grover Cleveland, aged nine, in an essay on the virtue of time well used

Stephen Grover Cleveland was born on March 18, 1837, in Caldwell, New Jersey. That year the United States was going through a difficult economic time, known as the Panic of 1837. Business everywhere was slow. People lost their jobs. Some families did not have enough money to pay their rent or buy food. The Cleveland family was already so poor that they barely noticed the panic.

Stephen's father, Richard Falley Cleveland, was a minister. The Cleveland family had some important ancestors. Some had served in the Revolutionary War (1775–1783). One helped the U.S. Constitution become law. Other Clevelands were famous clergymen, lawyers,

*Moses Cleaveland, one of many
distinguished Cleveland ancestors, was a
lawyer, surveyor, and brigadier general
in the Connecticut state militia.*

✧ ———————————

and businessmen. Moses
Cleaveland, who spelled the
family name differently from
the way Richard's immediate
family did, cofounded the city of
Cleaveland, Ohio. (The city dropped
the *a* from its name a decade before
Stephen was born.)

The Cleveland family was dedicated to ending slavery in
the United States. One Cleveland ancestor had tried to stop
slavery in the American colonies as early as 1797. Another
brought shipowners in Salem, Massachusetts, to court for
their role in the slave trade. Richard Cleveland made his par-
ents unhappy when he chose to go to Baltimore, Maryland,
to study for the ministry, because Baltimore accepted slavery.

In Baltimore Richard fell in love with a young woman
named Ann Neal. They were married in 1828, the same year
Richard became a minister. The couple began their life
together in Windham, Connecticut, where Richard accepted
a position as minister of a Congregationalist church. Ann
was in for some changes. First, her slave had to go. The people in Windham did not approve of slavery. They believed

that owning another human being was wrong. Ann also had to tone down her clothing. Churchgoers in strict, Puritan Connecticut saw the high fashions of Baltimore as sinful. Ann packed away her fancy clothes and jewelry and sent her slave back to Baltimore. She became a good minister's wife, and she even joined the fight against slavery.

Richard and Ann had nine children. Anna Neal and William Neal came first. Shortly after, Mary Allen and Richard Cecil arrived. Next was Stephen Grover, who later preferred to be called Grover. Margaret Louise, Lewis Frederick, Susan Sophia, and Rose Elizabeth followed him over the next few years.

Richard and Ann were strict with their children and taught them to take responsibility for their actions. Grover never forgot the lessons he learned at home. "Often as a boy," he said later, "I was [told by my parents] to get out of my warm bed at night, to hang up a hat or other garment which I had left on the floor." The

The Reverend Richard Cleveland

Reverend Cleveland taught his children that their lives must be guided by the true word of God, as expressed in the Bible. There was no middle ground between what was right and what was wrong.

When Grover was four years old, his father took over as minister of a church in Fayetteville, New York, a farming village near the Erie Canal. Grover went to public school in Fayetteville and then attended Fayetteville Academy, a private school for boys. But he got a better education at home. Under their father's watchful eye, the Cleveland children studied Latin, mathematics, and religion.

To earn extra money, the Cleveland boys took any jobs they could find. Sometimes they got up in the dark before school started to work on the canal, where they helped

Grover was not the only U.S. president to have worked on a canal as a youth. Above, James A. Garfield (president in 1881) urges horses to tow a canal boat from the shore of the Ohio and Pennsylvania Canal.

load and unload barges. They also cut wood and did other hard labor, such as hauling limestone. This rock, used in building, was the town's main export. Grover grew into a large, muscular teenager well suited for this type of work.

But life was not all work for the Cleveland children. Grover and William were known around town for pulling pranks not expected from sons of the local minister. One of their favorite tricks was to scare the townsfolk awake in the middle of the night by ringing the bell of the Fayetteville Academy. The Cleveland kids also swam in the local creeks, and Grover loved to fish on the banks of nearby Green Lake. The children had parties in their mother's kitchen, making taffy and popping corn.

MOVING ON

When Grover was fourteen, his father began to have health problems. Richard took a less tiring job in the offices of a religious organization in Clinton, New York, and moved the family again. The move was hard on Grover. He had to leave his friends and school behind. But the Cleveland children would have a better chance for a good education in Clinton. They could choose from the Clinton Liberal Institute, Hamilton College, and the Houghton Seminary.

While attending school at the Clinton Liberal Institute, Grover joined the debating society. This club split into teams and debated questions and ideas. The best argument won. One of the questions Grover debated was whether a lawyer should refuse to defend a client whom he knows is guilty. Fifteen-year-old Grover stated that it was wrong to defend a guilty person.

Grover's formal education ended in 1852. His father did not get better. He died of an infection in 1853. The family had no regular money coming in, so Grover and his brothers needed to find steady work. Although Grover had hoped to attend college, he knew that the family could not afford it. Instead, he took a job as a teacher at the New York Institution for the Blind in New York City.

AND GROWING UP

Grover's older brother William was already teaching at the Institution for the Blind. The school was run by the state of New York for poor children who were blind. The staff did

———————————— ✧ ————————————

The New York Institution for the Blind, founded in 1831, was the first school of its kind in the United States.

New York. Institution for the Blind.

not call the 116 young residents "students"—they referred to them as "inmates." Living conditions at the institution were sad. The halls and rooms were cold and damp. Rather than eat the food, which was terrible, some children went hungry.

Possibly the worst thing of all was the way the school's director made the children feel about themselves. He often told them that they deserved their difficulties, including blindness and poverty. The Cleveland brothers could do little to help the students, except to treat them kindly. William and Grover both thought of their time at the school as the darkest period of their lives.

In 1854 William went on with his studies to be a minister. Grover returned to his mother's home in Holland Patent, a village near Utica, New York, to think things over. He had decided to become a lawyer. He knew that the only way he could afford more schooling was to get a good job. Liking the fact that Cleveland, Ohio, was named for his ancestor, eighteen-year-old Grover headed there in 1855 to look for work. But on his way to Ohio, he stopped to visit an uncle who lived near Buffalo, New York. In Buffalo Grover found a better opportunity.

Grover's uncle had many business friends in Buffalo. He introduced Grover to the partners of a big law firm. They invited him to work in their offices. Grover not only helped the firm's lawyers but also read law books and paid attention to how things worked in court. In this way, he learned the law. At the same time, he was forming solid work habits. When one of the lawyers gave Grover a subject to learn about, he researched it with great care. He paid attention to even the smallest details. And he didn't stop until the job was done.

Buffalo, New York, had a strategic location on the Erie Canal, and the city grew rapidly after the canal was completed in 1825. On his way west, Cleveland stopped here to visit an uncle and decided to stay.

Located on the eastern end of Lake Erie, not far from Niagara Falls, Buffalo was a perfect place to do business. The city was connected to the south by the Erie Canal, which fed into the Hudson River. The Hudson linked Buffalo to New York City. Buffalo soon became a key place for trade between eastern cities and the western frontier. It was also the country's biggest center for flour making. The government seat of Erie County, Buffalo was connected by rail to Albany, the state capital.

Many German and Irish immigrants settled in Buffalo. The Germans built breweries, where they made beer. Every neighborhood had its own tavern, if not its own brewery. Men gathered in the bars after work to socialize, drink beer, and argue—often about politics. Cleveland, who liked beer and good company, hung out at the taverns and found friends among the local Democrats. Soon he was making political speeches. The taverns were a good place to practice giving speeches, because the people were friendly. Cleveland joined the Democratic Party sometime in the late 1850s. It was a smart move, because the Democrats ran the city of Buffalo.

THE YOUNG LAWYER AND POLITICIAN

Cleveland passed the New York State bar exam (a test for people who want to become lawyers) in 1859. This gave him the right to practice law in the state. He was twenty-two years old. He decided to stay on with the law firm as a senior clerk. During the next four years, he developed his own way to argue a case in the courtroom. He did not like to speak without planning first. He learned that he could deliver a very strong argument by memorizing what he was going to say—no script, no notes, no cue cards. His thorough research of a subject and ability to repeat a written text without a stammer made him a successful trial lawyer. He also became known for his honesty and principles in court. His success caught the attention of other lawyers, as well as politicians and newspaper editors. Everybody who worked with Cleveland praised him.

As a young man, Cleveland didn't imagine that he would become president of the United States. Still, he had dreams. His biggest dream was probably to be a judge on the U.S. Supreme Court. But he would be content with any judgeship. To become a judge, he knew he needed to be connected to one of the political parties, the Democrats or the new Republican Party. He had already joined the Democrats and was becoming well known in the party.

In 1862 Cleveland was elected supervisor of the city's second ward, or voting district. His hard work, honesty, and the backing of the Democratic Party got him the job of assistant district attorney for Erie County later that year.

The Civil War (1861–1865) had begun the year before Cleveland took public office, and young men from across New York were joining the Union army. The Conscription Act of 1863 required all men of Cleveland's age to serve in the army. When called, Cleveland hired someone else to join the army for him. This was a legal and common practice at the time. For $150, a young Polish immigrant took Cleveland's place.

THE U.S. CIVIL WAR

The Civil War was the deadliest conflict in U.S. history. More Americans died in that war than any other. The country was deeply divided over the issue of slavery, with Southern states supporting it and Northern states opposing it. When a group of Southern states (the Confederacy) threatened to leave the union of states, war broke out. The North called its army the Union army. The Southern force was the Confederate army.

It's not known exactly how many men served in the Civil War. Historians estimate that about 2,100,000 men fought for the Union army, while about 800,000 men served in the Confederate army. In some battles, as many as one of every four soldiers died. The casualty rate was so high that Civil War soldiers made their own tags to identify themselves if they were killed in battle.

It may have been Cleveland's sense of duty to his family that caused him to send another man to war in his place. Cleveland's mother and younger sisters were struggling to get by. Cleveland's older brother William was having trouble supporting his own family on a minister's income and could not help his mother and sisters. Cleveland's two younger brothers were serving in the Union army.

CHAPTER TWO

FAST TRACK TO
THE WHITE HOUSE

Public office is a public trust.
—Grover Cleveland's campaign slogan when
running for mayor of Buffalo, New York, 1881

Cleveland worked hard as assistant district attorney, and he was good at the job. To bring someone to trial, Cleveland first had to face a grand jury. A grand jury is a group of citizens who decide if enough evidence exists to bring a case to court. Cleveland got most of his cases to court, and then he won them.

To accomplish this, Cleveland sometimes went thirty-six hours at a time without sleep. He was at his desk at eight o'clock every morning. After a quick break for dinner, he went back to work at eight in the evening. Sometimes he stayed up until three in the morning to prepare for the next day's court battles. More than once, he argued four jury trials in a single day and won them all. He was tough on crime, a stance that made many people in the county respect him.

In 1865 the Democratic Party encouraged Cleveland to campaign for district attorney, and he made his first run for public office. But the Republican candidate won. Cleveland quickly shifted gears and started a law firm with two partners. One of his partners, Oscar Folsom, became his good friend. The law firm did well, and Cleveland's reputation grew. If he thought a client was lying, he would not take the case. He often argued cases that he believed in, even if the client could not afford to pay him.

In 1870 Cleveland ran as the Democratic candidate for county sheriff and won. This job paid very well. Rather than receiving a set salary, or amount of money, for his work, the sheriff collected fees. These could amount to more than $40,000 over a term of three years—the equivalent of $800,000 in current values. Erie County had the busiest jails in the state of New York. Buffalo had 673 taverns and many houses of prostitution. A fight might break out anywhere, anytime, among the canal workers, drifters, and sailors who hung around the streets. They often stole from others or even murdered people.

Erie County was in for a change with the office of sheriff in the hands of an honest man. First, Cleveland got rid of people who were cheating the county. He didn't care whether they were Democrat or Republican. Unlike earlier sheriffs, Cleveland also made sure that the county got the goods and services it paid for. He even checked the size of wood deliveries to see if they

As the sheriff of Erie County, Cleveland made certain that bills for county expenses, such as heating the courthouse (above), were fair.

contained less than what had been ordered. When he uncovered problems with the orders, the cost of wood to heat county buildings dropped. Twice he hanged murderers himself rather than pass on the unpleasant duty to others.

In 1872 Cleveland suffered a difficult personal loss. Two of his brothers were killed in a fire aboard a steamship headed for the Bahamas. The brothers left enough money to support their mother for the rest of her life, however.

After three years as sheriff, Cleveland turned down a second term. He'd had enough of rough company and wanted to work as a lawyer again. As his financial security grew, Cleveland spent more time on his social life. He had long been a regular at Buffalo's taverns. He enjoyed good beer, good food, and a good time. The food he liked best was sausages with sauerkraut. All of this could be found at his favorite hangout, Schenkelberger's.

At the tavern, he also found friends and at least one girlfriend, a widow named Maria Halpin. In 1874 Halpin gave birth to a son. She named him Oscar Folsom Cleveland, a choice that caused plenty of discussion. It is likely that both Folsom and Cleveland had been her lovers, but she declared Cleveland the father. Nobody ever learned whether she was right. However, Cleveland agreed that he might be the father and took responsibility.

He gave Halpin five hundred dollars to start a new life someplace other than Buffalo. He also paid a local orphanage five dollars a week for the boy's care. Soon a well-to-do family from western New York adopted the child. Cleveland probably never had contact with the boy after he was adopted. Halpin left town, as planned.

Some of Cleveland's friends thought that Folsom was the baby's father. They believed that Cleveland took the blame to protect his friend and partner, who was married. After Folsom was killed in a carriage accident the following July, the court asked Cleveland to manage his friend's business for his family. Over the years, Cleveland became very close friends with Folsom's wife, Emma, and their little girl, Frances.

Cleveland had gained more than one hundred pounds since arriving in Buffalo and was growing heavier. But with his six-foot-one height and perfect clothing, he always looked good. He had clear blue eyes, a well-shaped nose, and a full mustache. He never appeared in public unless dressed properly. That meant a black suit, white dress shirt, and top hat. Some people joked that this is what he wore even when he went fishing.

Cleveland hated the idea of exercise. But he was a good duck hunter and an excellent fisherman. By his mid-forties, Cleveland was happy with his life and didn't really want to return to public office. But the Democratic Party was about to shake things up for him.

MAYOR OF BUFFALO

After the Civil War, many people in American politics were crooked, or dishonest. Corruption was especially common during the two presidential terms of Ulysses S. Grant (1869–1877). Much of the dishonesty stemmed from the spoils system, in which political leaders gave contracts, jobs, and other favors to members of their own political party. The spoils system grew in the South after the war. It was also active in the North, especially in the major cities. Political parties and their bosses controlled almost all the business in every big city. The bosses handed out jobs and job contracts to their friends. The cities paid for the work, but the bosses' friends often didn't do it at all or did it badly.

One of the most powerful bosses was William M. Tweed. Known as Boss Tweed, he was the leader of the Tammany Society in New York City. This Democratic

This political cartoon shows Boss Tweed controlling the money in four cribs (safes). These cribs represent government funds at the city, county, state, and national level.

group held great power in New York City and throughout the state. Tweed and other party bosses paid people to vote for certain candidates at the polls. They also paid judges, politicians, and business leaders to make decisions that gave the society money and power.

Like other Americans, the citizens of Buffalo, New York, were tired of being cheated and wanted change. Local Democratic Party leaders urged Cleveland to run for mayor of Buffalo in 1881. He did and won in a landslide. In his first speech, he reminded city officials that the money they spent belonged to the public: "We are . . . trustees of our fellow citizens, holding their funds in a sacred trust."

He started saving the city money right away. First, he called off the party planned for his inauguration (the ceremony at which he was sworn into office). He was at his desk in the mayor's office the very next morning, and he expected other city workers to report to their jobs too. Workers could no longer take time off without a good reason. The city was not going to pay for anything that it did not receive, either. Cleveland ignored the city's spoils system. He read the bids (estimates of how much a job would cost) for city contracts and gave jobs to the best workers at the best price. He even cleaned up Buffalo's sewage and water problems.

Word about Cleveland's achievements spread across the state. This was a man who wanted to make government work for the people again. Many people began to think that if he could clean up Buffalo, he could clean up the whole state of New York. Why not make him the next governor?

On July 3, 1882, Cleveland made a speech at a celebration of Buffalo's history. The crowd cheered. Cleveland then hurried to Holland Patent to be with his mother, who was ill. He was at her bedside when she died on July 19 at age seventy-eight. Cleveland returned to his desk after her death and was surprised to learn that the newspapers wanted him to run for governor of New York.

New York was the richest and largest state in the Union in 1882. The Democrats knew that Cleveland could help fight corruption in the state. He agreed to run for governor if he could keep working as mayor of Buffalo as long as possible. He did not want to spend his time giving election speeches. Even though he did not campaign, Cleveland easily won the election. He had the support of Democrats and many Republican leaders. The state's newspapers had also backed him. He left Buffalo for the state capitol in Albany on the last day of 1882. Before going, he wrote to his brother William. He told his brother how much he was going to miss their mother. If she were still alive to guide him and pray for him, he said, he "should feel so much safer."

GOVERNOR OF NEW YORK
Cleveland moved into the governor's mansion in 1883. As soon as he arrived, he opened the grand house to the public. Sightseers were free to wander through the mansion.

────────── ✧

Governor Cleveland (right) meets with New York City police commissioner Theodore Roosevelt, another future president of the United States.

In his work, however, Cleveland was ready to say no to anyone. He did not care what the Democrats or Republicans wanted him to do. He did not hand out favors to friends. He did not pay attention to what people thought about him. When he gave someone a job, it was based on ability, not party membership. He went against both public opinion and Tammany Hall by vetoing, or preventing the passage of, a law that would cut the price of riding the trains in New York City. Local politicians and the Tammany Society wanted to pass the law to please the working people and get their votes.

Cleveland had studied the issue carefully. He decided that the law broke the city's original agreement to let the railroad set the fare price. People might be unhappy with his decision to veto the law, but he stood by it. Cleveland refused to look at the newspapers the next morning. But to everyone's surprise, the headlines praised him for his courage. He quickly won the voters' respect. National party leaders, who were searching for a Democratic candidate for president of the United States, noticed. But he had made enemies at Tammany Hall.

Cleveland stepped up his work routine. He worked every day, including Sundays. If he quit before midnight, he considered it a half day. He tried to save money for the state government in any way he could, including eating the food that was left over from state dinners. He took a day now and then to go fishing, however. On at least one of his fishing trips, he visited Oscar Folsom's widow and her daughter, Frances, who had grown up and was attending college.

Around this time, Cleveland's relationship with Frances became romantic. When she went back to school for her last year, Cleveland sent her gifts of flowers and a puppy. Frances's friends spread rumors about her seeing an older gentleman. The couple remained silent about their feelings.

During her last year in college, Frances Folsom received many romantic gifts from Cleveland.

To relax when he was at home, Cleveland read, memorized poetry, and played poker. Sometimes he went to the Roman Catholic cathedral to pray. He was not a Catholic, but the church was close to his office.

PRESIDENTIAL CANDIDATE

The Democrats had not had a president in the White House since James Buchanan. President Buchanan served from 1857 to 1861, just before the start of the Civil War. For years the party had been split over slavery. Northern Democrats opposed it. Southern Democrats were for it. But most voters forgot about the Northern Democrats and thought of the Democrats as pro-slavery. The result was a weakened and unpopular national party. The Republicans took advantage of this weakness, taking every opportunity to claim that the Democrats had started the war and been disloyal to the Union. In this way, they kept control of the White House.

Until the mid-nineteenth century, party members had more power than the candidates themselves in U.S. presidential elections. In fact, party members often gave speeches for the candidates. The parties held parades and other festive events just before they met at their conventions, the huge gatherings where they decided whom they were going to support for office.

Two weeks before the 1884 Democratic Convention, Cleveland wrote to New York's Democratic leader, Daniel Manning. In the letter, Cleveland stated that he did not have even "a particle of ambition to be President of the United States." But party officials saw him as an ideal candidate. In just one year as New York's governor,

Cleveland had changed the way the state's jobs were given out. He put rules in place to improve the insurance industry. He watched every public dollar that was spent. He made sure that work projects were done right. Concerned about public complaints, he created a court where they could be heard. The fact that Cleveland had a bad relationship with the Tammany bosses increased his appeal to voters outside New York. Most Americans didn't like the political "machines" that controlled government.

This political cartoon makes fun of the Tammany ring. It pictures the way members of the Tammany ring avoided justice. Each man points a finger of blame at the man to his right.

Cleveland wanted to be honest with the Democratic leaders. Before they chose him for office, he told them that Maria Halpin had accused him of fathering her child. They were not worried.

The Republicans decided not to back Chester Arthur, the current president. Although he was a Republican, Arthur wanted to get rid of the spoils system and make other changes that party leaders did not approve. They chose James Gillespie Blaine as their candidate instead.

✧ ————————————

While campaigning for the U.S. presidency in 1884, Cleveland visits his adopted hometown of Buffalo, New York. Residents show their support with a parade and fireworks.

Blaine had been in politics a long time. He had served three terms as Speaker of the U.S. House of Representatives and one term as a senator. A great public speaker, Blaine knew politics inside and out. He was also a snappy dresser. To mainstream Republicans, he looked like a good choice.

Not all party members agreed, however. Some Republicans wanted to reform the political system, ending the spoils system and other corrupt practices. These Republicans became known as Mugwumps, an Algonquin Indian word meaning "chiefs." Blaine had used the spoils system all his political life. In 1869, while Speaker of the House, he had been accused of doing favors for the Little Rock and Fort Smith Railroad. The railroad gave Blaine a lot of money in return.

The Mugwumps refused to back Blaine. They wanted an honest candidate, no matter what his party. As far as they were concerned, Grover Cleveland was a better choice. Most Democrats agreed, and the party selected him as their candidate for president, along with Indiana governor Thomas Hendricks as his running mate for the vice-presidential seat.

CHAPTER THREE

"MA! MA! WHERE'S MY PA?"

Whatever you do, tell the truth.
—telegram from Grover Cleveland to Democratic
Party officials on July 23, 1883

In 1884 neither the Democrats nor the Republicans paid much attention to the country's growing problems as they started their fight for the White House. Times were changing in the United States. Many Americans had moved from small farming towns to large cities. They came to work in factories and other big businesses. Immigrants also flooded into the cities. In 1850, 2.25 million people had arrived in the United States as immigrants. In 1880 nearly 7 million came. Cities and states faced many new problems and challenges.

THE OVERLOOKED ISSUES
The tremendous population growth put a strain on cities. Many of the new residents were poor. They crowded into the cheapest housing they could find. This created health and

safety problems, such as poor sanitation and outbreaks of illness. As the number of workers grew, working conditions got worse. U.S.-born citizens competed with immigrants for jobs. Often the established residents treated the newcomers badly. No effective, large-scale programs, such as Social Security or welfare, existed to help the poor.

Slaves freed by the Civil War needed to find work too. Many could not get jobs because of racial discrimination or lack of skills. In the South, African Americans had been targeted by racist groups such as the Ku Klux Klan (KKK), whose white-hooded members terrorized black communities.

Farmers were slipping into debt. Settlers and gold miners were taking the Native Americans' land on the Great Plains, west of the Mississippi River. When the Native Americans fought back, the government forced them onto reservations, areas of land set aside for them. Many times, clashes between Native Americans and soldiers or settlers turned violent.

These social and economic problems were very difficult to solve. The political parties turned their attention to easier issues. The Democrats wanted lower taxes—called tariffs—on goods imported from other countries. Lower tariffs would make imports cheaper to buy. This meant that U.S. goods would sell for lower prices to compete with imports. The Democrats believed that working people would benefit, because they could more easily afford to buy the goods they needed. The Democratic candidate, Grover Cleveland, also promised to make the government more honest.

The Republicans wanted higher tariffs on imported goods to keep the price of U.S. goods high. They said this was good for workers. When U.S. factories were selling their products at higher prices, companies could afford to hire more workers and pay them higher wages. Many Republicans didn't see a need to clean up the way government worked.

Except for the tariffs and Cleveland's ideas about government reform, the two parties' plans were very similar. In the campaign, they focused on personal issues instead of public problems.

TRUTH AND LIES

The 1884 election was one of the dirtiest presidential campaigns in U.S. history. Finding no political issues to use against Cleveland, the Republicans headed for lower ground. They came up with gold when they learned about his affair with Maria Halpin.

The Reverend George H. Ball, a Buffalo pastor, broke the Maria Halpin story to a Buffalo newspaper. Ball was a Republican with a good sense of timing. The Democrats had just chosen Cleveland as their candidate when the newspaper ran Ball's story under the headline, "A Terrible Tale: A Dark Chapter in a Public Man's Life." The minister charged Cleveland with seducing a young woman of high morals who gave birth to his son. Ball declared that the Halpin affair was part of a pattern in Cleveland's personal life. He said he could provide "more proof of [shameful actions] too horrible to relate and too vile to be readily believed."

Other newspapers instantly reported that Cleveland had had a child outside of marriage. The Republican Party made sure that the story was told and retold. It became the subject of many popular political cartoons. One of the cartoons was captioned, "Ma! Ma! Where's My Pa?" The Republicans turned this into a campaign slogan.

During Cleveland's campaign for president in 1884, many political cartoons took up the claim that he had a child outside of marriage.

✧

Cleveland had never kept his affair with Maria Halpin a secret. He had told Democratic Party officials about it. The Democrats who liked him said that his offense was minor, a mistake that lots of men made. Some of Cleveland's supporters had been accused of similar behavior themselves. Among them was a well-known minister, Henry Ward Beecher. Beecher claimed that if every man who was guilty of the same sin voted for Cleveland, he'd win in a landslide.

Presidents and the Press

From the start of American politics, journalists viewed the president as fair game for criticism and comment. George Washington declared after his first election, "The editors of the different Gazettes . . . [should be] . . . publishing the debates in Congress rather than stuffing their papers with . . . [scandal]." And the stories aimed at him were mild compared to those written about later presidents.

During Thomas Jefferson's run for president, newspapers wrote that he had had children with one of his slaves. When Andrew Jackson ran for office, the press went after his wife, Rachel. She had been married before her marriage to Jackson and had lived with him while waiting for the divorce from her first husband. Although these events had taken place more than thirty-five years earlier, the editor of the *Cincinnati Gazette* wrote a series of stories on the Jacksons' marriage. He called the couple "a convicted adulteress and her [lover] husband." It was said that Rachel died from a heart attack after reading one of these stories in a pamphlet. She was buried in the gown she had bought for her husband's victory party.

The newspaper stories about Abraham Lincoln were especially cruel. Lincoln, who drank nothing stronger than lemonade, was often reported to be an alcoholic. He was described as a "third-rate lawyer" with "a face like a gorilla."

The Cleveland-Blaine scandals came at a time when newspapers were competing furiously for sales. City newspapers printed headlines that would sell. Smaller newspapers copied what the big newspapers said. They didn't worry much about checking facts.

Cleveland was also said to have been involved with many women. His enemies spread rumors that he planned to have women visit him in the White House. Most of these attacks seemed to come from the same source, George Ball. The Tammany Society also spread rumors to damage Cleveland's reputation in New York.

Cleveland kept calm. When asked by Democratic leaders what they should say about the scandal, he simply told them to tell the truth. He added that at no time did he ever use the governor's mansion to entertain lady friends, nor did he plan to invite women to the White House. From this point on, Cleveland remained silent on the issue. He stayed at the governor's mansion and made only a few public appearances during the campaign.

The Democrats did what they could to keep Blaine's railroad scandal alive. Blaine protested, claiming that he had not taken money to help the railroad when he was Speaker of the House. Yet the *New York Times* had printed a letter in which he admitted the crime. At the end of the letter, he had written, "Burn this letter."

People from the Democratic campaign dug up some "dirt" about Blaine's personal life as well. The Democrats looked up the date of Blaine's marriage and compared it with the date of the birth of his first child. The child had been born just three months after the wedding. Blaine got the nickname Slippery Jim when he claimed that he and his wife had been married twice. He said that their first marriage had taken place well before the birth of their child. The Democrats found no public record of a first marriage, however.

Cleveland felt that going public with Blaine's railroad deal was fair. But he wanted no part in the personal attacks. He was especially aware of the pain that the newspaper stories were causing Blaine's wife. He told his campaign people to stop repeating the story about her marriage date. The Democrats then came up with a slogan of their own: "Blaine! Blaine! James G. Blaine! The Continental Liar from the state of Maine!"

The Republicans headed for even lower ground. They printed fliers saying that all the Cleveland brothers of draft age during the Civil War had avoided their duty. Further, the man that Grover Cleveland had sent to fight in his place had been badly wounded. They said that the man had asked Cleveland for help and had been turned away. The Republicans spread the fliers throughout the country, and many newspapers published the charges.

The Democrats easily proved that these accusations were false. Army records showed that two of the Cleveland brothers had gone to war. They fought with honor and were promoted in rank to lieutenants. Records also indicated that Cleveland's paid replacement spent most of the war serving in a military hospital, due to a back injury. Despite these records, "Draft Dodging Grover!" joined the list of Republican campaign slogans. (A draft dodger is an insulting name for someone who avoids serving in the army.)

THE RESULTS

Cleveland's retreat to the governor's mansion and silence during the campaign turned out to be good strategies for dealing with the charges made against him. Blaine was by far the better speaker and debater. But Cleveland refused to face him in a public debate. To win the election, Blaine believed he needed to win New York. He took off on a tiring speaking tour across the state.

Blaine did not get back to New York City until the end of October. The city was alive with the campaign. Both parties held long parades through the streets day and night and threw noisy political rallies. Party members gave speeches in support of their candidate. Some speakers got careless with their words, however. If Blaine hadn't been so tired, he might have stopped the Reverend Samuel Burchard before he got up to speak. Burchard blasted the Democrats and called them the party of "Rum, Romanism [Roman Catholicism], and Rebellion."

This slogan was an insult to Irish Americans and other Catholic groups. Newspapers quickly reported the speech. With this mistake, Blaine lost many votes—nearly half a million Irish-born people lived in New York City alone.

A few days later, on November 4, 1884, Grover Cleveland was elected the twenty-second president of the United States. The election was one of the closest in the history of the U.S. presidency. Cleveland won his home state of New York by only twelve hundred votes. Close or not, the Democrats celebrated their first presidential victory since 1857. In answer to the Republicans' "Ma! Ma! Where's My Pa?" Democrats came back with, "Gone to the White House, Ha! Ha! Ha!"

——————————— ✧
The Reverend Samuel Burchard

President Cleveland stands at the front of a flag-draped platform at the U.S. Capitol at his inauguration on March 4, 1885.

CHAPTER FOUR

WELCOME TO
THE WHITE HOUSE

*[Serving as president is]
a dreadful self-afflicted [punishment]
for the good of my country.*
—Grover Cleveland in a letter to a friend,
November 18, 1884

Grover Cleveland left Albany, New York, for Washington, D.C., two days before he was sworn in as president on March 4, 1885. Keeping to his strict rule never to accept personal favors while in public office, he turned down the free ride offered by several railroads. He traveled on a train hired by the Democratic Party and paid part of the cost himself. Although President Arthur invited him to stay at the White House, Cleveland checked into a hotel. He did not want to trouble the outgoing president.

Cleveland had stayed in the governor's mansion during most of the campaign. He had never been interested in traveling outside his own circle of work and home. So when he arrived in Washington for his inauguration, most people in the capital were seeing Cleveland in person for the first time. One senator, who later came to greatly admire Cleveland, described him as heavy and rough looking. But the audience who heard the new president speak that day must have been impressed. Using the skills he'd learned when training to be a lawyer, he gave the speech from memory. He had no need for notes. He simply clasped his hands behind his back, looked straight out at the audience, and gave his speech perfectly.

The speech itself held no surprises. It was clear from the start what Cleveland planned to do. He intended to manage the public's money carefully, give out jobs based on ability and experience rather than favoritism, and stay friendly to business. He promised to put the interests of the American people first. This included the Native Americans—Cleveland said he would try to make up for the harsh treatment and broken promises they had experienced in the past. African Americans, he declared, had nothing to fear. He would see that they received fair and equal treatment, as set out in the Constitution.

In his inaugural speech, Cleveland said that he looked forward to peaceful relations with foreign nations, but he vowed to be careful in any agreements he made with them. He looked to the Constitution to define his role as president and believed that his main duty was to carry out the laws passed by Congress. He told the audience that he would not be afraid to use his power to veto, or kill, any laws that were not in the interests of the American people. The whole speech took about fifteen minutes.

That spring Cleveland had more than just his important new work responsibilities on his mind. Soon after he took office, he asked Frances Folsom to marry him. She agreed to a wedding set for the following spring. They tried to keep their plans secret. But that summer, the newspapers caught on. The president began to dread the fun the press was going to have at his expense.

SETTLING IN

A typical day for Cleveland was very different from that of later presidents. Trying to improve the U.S. government job system—his main campaign promise—took a great deal of time. He tried to hire people based on their skills and qualifications rather than their political party. He personally sorted through thousands of applications just for jobs with the post office.

Cleveland also spent many hours talking to politicians and private citizens. Three times a week, he held a public reception. During these gatherings, anyone, including

——————— ✧
Cleveland (left) greets a little girl at a White House reception.

tourists, could speak to him or shake his hand. Cleveland was often on his feet mixing with the crowd the entire time. He met with his cabinet members (his top advisers) and other officials in person.

In addition, Cleveland received many letters every day. Daniel Scott Lamont, the president's personal secretary, sorted through the mail. Cleveland answered many of them in his own handwriting.

Cleveland showed his warmth in a response to a little girl who remembered his birthday:

> *I thought my birthday would be a pretty dull affair, and I didn't suppose that anyone would care enough about such a dreadfully old man to notice the occasion. But when I read the nice little message. . . you sent, I began to think that birthdays were pretty good things after all.*

He also wrote to the many people who asked for money or other favors. Sometimes he sent them checks. He wrote to one family, "I hope [the money I am sending] will add to your comfort and that of the young triplets. I am so unaccustomed to matters of the kind that I must ask to be excused from the attempt to give names to the three little girls."

Cleveland and his assistant, William Sinclair, practically ran the White House by themselves. They had only a small staff of servants and clerks to help. The president himself sometimes answered the door when the bell rang. He also answered the White House telephone.

The White House was open to the public. Even though two previous presidents had been assassinated, only a few detectives were assigned to keep the president safe. (The Secret Service was not used to protect the president until after 1901, when William McKinley was assassinated.)

Cleveland kept track of all White House expenses. He paid for any personal costs from his own money. His sister Rose filled the role of official hostess. A teacher and author, she had more modern ideas than her brother. For example, she thought women should have the same rights as men. She also thought that the government should have programs to help the poor.

✧ ————

Rose Elizabeth Cleveland served for fifteen months as the White House hostess for her older brother but was not fond of greeting people and making small talk.

Rose was not really cut out to be a hostess, however. A lot of people thought she was downright unfriendly. She got bored at social gatherings and stared into space. She once admitted that she liked to silently practice verb forms of the Greek language instead of talk to guests.

As he always had, Cleveland worked long hours. Usually he was at his desk from early morning until as late as three o'clock the following morning. Once in a while, he took time to go fishing. But he did not use the presidential yacht for such outings. He loved baseball but never went to a game. He was worried that the public might think he was wasting his time.

THE SPOILS SYSTEM
Before he took office, Cleveland had given his friends and fellow Democrats a warning. They were not to ask him for

✧ ————————
From the start, Cleveland put in long hours in his White House office.

jobs or other favors. They ignored him and began to request jobs, appointments, money, and favors even before he left the governor's mansion in Albany.

As much as Cleveland disliked the spoils system, even he could not get rid of it entirely. Important members of both parties pushed him to keep promises they had made before the election. Cleveland had to face facts. He needed to fill about one hundred thousand government jobs fast. (Many of these jobs were for postmasters. At the time, this job was a political appointment.) Cleveland hired only those who could do the job well. But if two people had the same abilities, he chose the Democrat out of loyalty to his party. As a result, many Republican government workers lost their jobs to those with connections to the Democratic Party. But fewer Democrats were hired than people expected. In the end, Cleveland did not satisfy either those who wanted the spoils system changed or those who did not.

MONEY TROUBLE

A month before he was sworn in as president in 1885, Cleveland had written a public letter to Congress asking members to get rid of a law that he and many others felt could ruin the economy. The law, passed in 1878, was called the Bland-Allison Act. It stated that the government had to start using silver coins. Silver miners in the American West and others connected to the silver industry liked the law. They knew that if the government had to use silver, its value would go up. Others also supported the use of silver because they thought it would help the economy.

Before the silver law, the United States was on the gold standard. Under the gold standard, every dollar used in the

Workers inside a U.S. Treasury vault count silver coins in the late 1800s.

◇ ————————

country was backed by a set amount of gold in the U.S. Treasury. Anyone could trade in coins or paper money for real gold. This system is also called a sound money policy.

Cleveland wanted to return to the gold standard. He believed that silver was upsetting the economy. Most business owners, bankers, and other wealthy people agreed with him. Most Republicans and many Democrats, including farmers, did not agree. They believed that silver coins would make U.S. currency less valuable. In turn, U.S. goods (including farm products) would be cheaper to buy than foreign-made goods.

In 1885 the silver supporters in Congress won, refusing to overturn the Bland-Allison Act. But the issue continued to be debated throughout Cleveland's term as president. Meanwhile, since gold was worth more than silver, Americans and others were trading their silver dollars for gold. The Treasury was drained of gold and the economy was getting shaky.

STOLEN LANDS

In his inaugural speech, Cleveland had promised to keep Native American lands from being stolen. Throughout U.S. history, the government had set aside land for Native Americans many times. Each time, settlers, ranchers, gold miners, and others had gradually taken it over. One Native American nation had a saying: "Heaven [is] the place where white men lie no more."

Early in his term, Cleveland took action against two thousand settlers who had moved illegally onto Native American lands. He sent U.S. marshals to move the settlers. But even though he sent an additional eighteen companies of army soldiers, the settlers resisted. This was a sign of just how difficult a problem Cleveland had on his hands.

WORKER UNREST

Cleveland faced another problem as he started his presidency. On Cleveland's very first day in the White House, more than fifty thousand coal miners were on strike. This meant that the workers refused to work until they got better conditions on the job. The miners were part of a labor union, a large group of workers whose leaders demand fair treatment from their employers. By sticking together, or organizing, union members gained some power over the owners or employers in an industry. For example, the union could call a strike. A strike could shut down a factory, mine, railroad, or other business. Such union actions could even ruin the owner financially.

THE RISE OF LABOR UNIONS

In the years following the Civil War, the United States had shifted from an economy based on farming and small shops to an industrial economy based on factory manufacturing and transportation. By the time Cleveland took office in 1885, the number of industrial laborers in the United States had grown from fewer than three million to around nine million. In addition, the huge jump in urban populations created a growing pool of unskilled workers, including immigrants, women, and children.

With a steady supply of new workers available, manufacturers had little reason to improve working conditions. Laborers were expected to work sixty hours a week at low wages, under crowded, unhealthy, and often unsafe conditions. Workers could be fired, laid off, or forced to work overtime. They had no health or accident insurance. If they got sick or hurt, they had to pay for medical care out of their own pockets or go without, and they were not paid for any days of work they missed.

Ordinary workers noticed the huge differences between their lives and those of their bosses. While the factory managers and owners had large, fancy houses, workers often lived in dark, broken-down apartments called tenements. These were located in the worst parts of the city. The tenements were usually full of lice and rats. Families might live in a single room, without a bathroom or kitchen or indoor lighting. Because people cooked wherever they could and used candles or lanterns for lighting, the apartments often caught fire. Crime was another common problem.

As workers watched the gap between themselves and rich people widen, they started to fight back. They formed labor unions, such as the Knights of Labor and the American

Business owners and managers lived in enormous homes staffed by servants, such as this one in Narragansett, Rhode Island. The wage workers they employed lived in small, crowded apartments. The contrast between these lifestyles was sharp.

Federation of Labor (AFL). In 1885 unions called more strikes than ever before in U.S. history.

Many employers hated the unions and fought hard to keep them from growing in number and power. Employers used various tactics to keep the unions from calling a strike. For example, a company might fire all the workers before or during a strike and hire new people in their place. Because both sides had so much at stake during a strike, strikes often turned violent.

President Cleveland was aware that employers often treated workers and their unions badly. He tried to encourage business owners to respect the unions and talk to workers about their problems.

In April 1886, the Knights of Labor workers' union called a strike. Ten thousand railroad workers walked off the job. This stopped trains on sixty thousand miles of track. All trains west of the Mississippi River screeched to a stop. The strike kept farmers from getting their goods to market. It kept cities from getting food and other things they needed.

The railroad owners brought the problem to Congress. Cleveland sent a message to Congress saying that he could understand why the union had called the strike. He thought the workers had a fair complaint—the owners had tried to break the union by firing its members. Cleveland reminded Congress of the value of the working person. He advised lawmakers to form a group to look into labor problems and find peaceful ways to solve them.

✧ ———————

Striking railroad workers try to prevent a train from leaving East Saint Louis, Illinois, during their 1886 strike. U.S. marshals hold them back.

A group of the sort Cleveland had in mind might have prevented the Haymarket Riot in Chicago, Illinois. In May 1886, fifteen hundred workers from a farm machinery company gathered in Chicago's Haymarket Square. When police tried to hurry them away, a bomb blew up. At least fifty policemen were hurt badly. Eight were killed. As a result, four of the union leaders were hanged and others were put in jail. The Haymarket Riot was a setback for the labor unions. It made people afraid to join them. It also made factory owners more willing to join together to fight the workers. Cleveland was frustrated that his proposal for a labor board had been ignored.

———————————— ✧ ————————————

Like the railroad workers striking in 1886, the farm machine workers who gathered at Haymarket Square in Chicago, Illinois, in May of that year were Knights of Labor union members.

CHAPTER FIVE

WEDDING VOWS AND PRESIDENTIAL VETOES

I am to be married on Wednesday evening at seven o'clock at the White House to Miss Folsom.

—handwritten wedding invitation that Cleveland sent to cabinet members and friends, May 1886

Cleveland's marriage to Frances Folsom was planned for June 2, 1886. The president did not look forward to the circus the press would make of his wedding. He tried hard to keep reporters away from Frances. He wrote to his sister Mary in March 1886, "The quicker it can be done the better." After his dealings with the press during his presidential campaign, he thought of newspaper reporters as a "dirty gang" that had treated him badly.

The wedding took place in the White House Blue Room. Composer John Philip Sousa conducted as the U.S. Marine Corps Band played the *Wedding March*. A candlelight dinner was held in the State Dining Room. Many famous people sent their good wishes. Even Queen Victoria of Great Britain sent a friendly note to wish the couple well.

The Clevelands slipped away from the wedding party to honeymoon at a rented cottage in Deer Park, Maryland. They could see the Blue Ridge Mountains from the window. Cleveland thought that the press would leave them alone, at least for his honeymoon.

The cottage was supposed to be in a secret location. But when Cleveland opened the cottage door the morning after his wedding, he found reporters hiding behind the trees. He raged against the reporters. They had even peeked under the lids of the dishes left on the step from the

Grover Cleveland was the first president to marry in the White House.

honeymoon meals. They wanted to report to the nation what the Clevelands were eating.

THE HAPPY COUPLE

Cleveland and his new bride were an unlikely pair. By the time of his marriage, Cleveland was forty-nine years old and weighed over three hundred pounds. His nieces and nephews called him Uncle Jumbo. Many of his White House friends and fellow politicians just called him the Big One. Frances was only twenty-one. She was educated, fluent in French and German. She was stylish, social, and loved parties. Cleveland hated all formal social gatherings.

Despite their differences, the Clevelands seemed to have had a very happy marriage. Frances put up with traits in her husband that other women might have found difficult. For instance, she did not seem to mind that he worked constantly. Cleveland was by no means modern in his thinking about women's role in society. He described a good wife as "a woman who loves her husband and her country with no desire to run either."

Still, Cleveland did not keep Frances from doing what she wanted. She vowed at their wedding to love, honor, comfort, and keep her husband—but not to obey him, as most brides at the time did. The press made a big deal out of this, but Cleveland did not.

During their marriage, Frances Cleveland pursued her own interests. She supported the Woman's Christian Temperance Union (WCTU), a group that spoke out about the dangers of the use of alcohol, drugs, and tobacco. Some WCTU members believed that the sale of alcohol should be against the law. Frances worked for other social causes as well. She was especially interested in help-ing poor women and working women. She held one of her two weekly receptions for the public on Saturdays so that working women could attend. To assist young black women in need, Frances started the Washington House for Friendless Colored Girls. Believing that women should have the same opportunity for higher education as men, she helped to found the New Jersey College for Women.

Frances also enjoyed her role as White House hostess. And the public adored her. They watched her every move, and women often copied her hairstyle and clothing. The press reported everything they could learn about the charming young Mrs. Cleveland.

——————— ✧
As First Lady, Frances
Cleveland set fashions
for women all over the
country.

Civil War veterans and families seek help from a private charity in New York City. The number of veterans needing assistance overwhelmed city agencies. To win votes, politicians granted many federally funded pensions to veterans. But Cleveland vetoed any that seemed dishonest.

CIVIL WAR PENSIONS

Cleveland's private life was peaceful. But his relationship with Congress was not. One issue that the president and members of Congress fought over was the government's pension plan for soldiers. In 1862 the federal government had set up a program to give a yearly payment, or pension, to poor Union soldiers who had served with honor in the Civil War. If the soldier was dead, the money was sent to his family.

Although the war had been over for twenty years, Congressmen were sending President Cleveland bills to sign that granted new pensions. The lawmakers never checked to see if the person asking for a pension really qualified for it. Granting pensions was an easy way to get more votes in their home states.

THE PRESIDENTIAL VETO

Congress sends bills, or proposals for a new law, to the president. The U.S. Constitution gives the president four ways to respond:

- Sign the bill, making it a law.
- Hold the bill for ten days when Congress will still be in session. This means that the president doesn't approve of parts of the bill but wants to see other parts become law.
- Hold the bill for ten days when Congress is about to close its session and cannot pass it. This means that there are too many things about the bill that the president doesn't like to let it become a law. This action is sometimes called a pocket veto.
- Veto the bill, which kills it outright, along with any additions made by different members of Congress.

The Constitution gives the president the veto—which means "forbid" in Latin—to keep power balanced within the government. But to make sure the president doesn't have too much power, the Constitution limits the veto. If two-thirds of the Congress agree, they can override, or ignore, the president's veto.

Some presidents don't veto any bills at all. Cleveland vetoed 584 bills in all. Although he vetoed more bills in his first term of office than any of the twenty-one presidents before him had in a single term, he wasn't the top veto president. That honor goes to Franklin Delano Roosevelt, who issued 635 vetoes during his three full terms in office (1933–1945).

In six months, Cleveland studied 4,127 pension bills sent to him by Congress. He vetoed the ones that seemed dishonest, such as pensions for soldiers who had run away from their units. He turned down a pension for a woman who said her husband had died a war hero. Cleveland found out that the man had never fought in the war. In fact, he had choked to death in 1880 while drunk. The president also vetoed a pension for a man who had received his wounds at a Fourth of July party twenty-three years before he went to war.

Many people who had served in the Union army were angry when they heard about the president's vetoes. The veterans called Cleveland a draft dodger and said he didn't care about them.

Cleveland actually granted more pensions than he vetoed. And he had done his research so carefully that he knew just what the pensions had cost. From 1861 to 1887, the U.S. government had given $808,624,811.51 to veterans. (That would be equal to more than $15 billion in 2005.)

MONOPOLIES AND TARIFFS

As Cleveland sorted through the war pensions, another problem was developing. The rich owners of big companies were banding together to control the market for their goods. This kind of agreement among several businesses in the same industry is called a monopoly. As a group, the company owners agreed to lower their prices for a set length of time. Smaller companies that tried to compete would eventually be forced out of business because they could not match the low prices offered by the big companies. With the smaller companies out of business, the big companies could raise their prices as high as they wanted. They could also lower the wages they paid, since fewer companies were around to hire workers.

With such power, a monopoly could push Congress into passing laws that raised tariffs on goods imported from other countries. Imported goods with high tariffs cost more, so fewer buyers could afford them. This made it harder for foreign companies to compete with an American monopoly.

In 1887 Cleveland made it illegal for the railroad industry to form monopolies. He signed the Interstate Commerce Act. If correctly enforced, the law would keep the railroads from working together to fix prices.

In this political cartoon, a long, strong arm reaches out of the White House to grab a rich railroad tycoon. The arm is Cleveland's 1887 Interstate Commerce Act, designed to end price-fixing among railroads.

Cleveland strongly believed that a major cause of poverty in the United States was the high tariffs on imports. With high tariffs in place, U.S. producers did not have to lower their prices. Cleveland argued that high tariffs were unfair to poor citizens.

Cleveland was very worried about the high tariffs set by Congress. He was so worried that he did something no other president had done before. He devoted his whole 1887 yearly message to Congress to the subject of tariffs. (Since the 1930s, this message has been called the State of the Union address.) All Cleveland talked about was how the high tariffs were hurting the poor.

The speech pleased Republicans. They knew that with such a strong stand on tariffs, Cleveland could not win a second term in office. Most workers voted the way their employers told them to, and few employers supported lower tariffs.

CHAPTER SIX

THE GIFT OF CITIZENSHIP

*Watch well, then, this high office, the most
precious possession of American citizenship.*
—Grover Cleveland, 1887

Grover Cleveland considered it a great honor to be a
U.S. citizen. The Constitution gives each citizen basic
human rights, which can never be taken away. But good
citizens earn these rights by supporting the government
and following its laws. In Cleveland's view, good citizens
also spoke English and kept the same social practices as
white, mainstream Americans. That is, citizens needed to
blend in with other Americans. They should live in the
same kinds of houses. They should send their children to
school and church. And they should also dress and wear
their hair in similar ways. This way, he believed, all
Americans could work together toward the same goals
and be at peace with their fellow citizens.

THE DAWES ACT

During Cleveland's first term as president, thousands of white settlers were moving west, looking for land and opportunities. It didn't matter that much of the land belonged to Native Americans. While Cleveland tried to hold back the tide of people moving west, government agents warned that an Indian war was starting in the Southwest. The Apache leader Geronimo and a group of followers began raiding white settlements in Arizona and New Mexico. On April 20, 1885, Cleveland sent out

Geronimo led his warriors in many surprise raids on white settlers in the Southwest as early as the 1870s. But as he prepared a major strike against the settlements in 1885, Cleveland used force to stop it.

U.S. troops to stop the attacks. By July the army had captured the Apaches and placed them under guard in Florida.

Cleveland still hoped that he could give each tribal group an area of land that could not be taken away. But he was a realist. He knew that the land would have to be measured in the white man's way, as a plot with clearly drawn borders. The open stretches of land and hunting grounds where native people could move freely were gone forever.

Cleveland's plan was simple. The government would give all Native Americans a piece of land that they could farm. In 1887 Senator Henry L. Dawes brought a bill to the Senate that put this plan into action. Known as the Dawes Act, the law assured every Native American of a plot of land as well as U.S. citizenship. Unfortunately, the law did not protect the large amount of land that was left over after the government assigned the plots. The government put the extra land up for sale, and white settlers quickly snapped it up. In addition, some native people sold their land to whites.

The Dawes Act meant the end of a way of life for many Native Americans. Some tribes were already farming in permanent communities. But other tribes, such as the Sioux, were hunters. They had always followed the buffalo across the land, moving to different places throughout the year. Such traditions didn't matter to the U.S. government, which decided that all Native Americans would be farmers with set boundaries to their land. This way the government thought it could regulate Native Americans' property and rights.

Sitting Bull expressed little regard for white people. Still, he appeared to feel honored that President Grover Cleveland once shook his hand and treated him with respect.

✧ ─────────────

Most Native Americans did not like Cleveland's plan. They did not want to give up their way of life, and they didn't care about being U.S. citizens. Sitting Bull, the great Sioux leader, fought back when the government tried to confine his people and force them to give up their language and culture. Sitting Bull declared, "If the Great Spirit had wanted me to be a white man, he would have made me one."

President Cleveland saw it differently. He believed that unless Native Americans adapted to European American society, they could not survive. For this reason, he supported a movement to send Native American children to govern-ment-run boarding schools, away from their homes and

families. There the children learned to speak English. The
teachers made them dress and behave like European
Americans. They cut the children's long hair so they would
look more like white children. Many Native Americans who
attended these schools later got good jobs and succeeded in
the white world. But in the process, some lost their native
languages and cultures.

To Cleveland, this loss was not a bad thing. He ruled
that classes at the boarding schools be taught only in
English. He wanted Native American students to forget
what he called their own "barbarous [uncivilized] language."

*In this photograph from the late 1800s, students at Pierre Indian School in
Pierre, South Dakota, wear European American hairstyles and clothing.*

EQUAL AND EXACT JUSTICE

Black Americans had greeted Grover Cleveland's election as president with caution. The Democratic Party had placed him in office. In the South, this was the party that had defended the right to own slaves.

Many southern whites resented the fact that blacks were not only free but were citizens with the same rights as whites. Some white southerners joined groups like the KKK. It treated freed slaves brutally, burning down their homes and taking part in lynchings (hangings) throughout the South. KKK members vowed that they would never travel in the same trains with blacks, attend the same churches, or send their children to the same schools. To them, the South belonged to whites.

———————————— ✧ ————————————

In this illustration from the late 1800s, Ku Klux Klansmen masked in white hoods attack a black family in their home.

Cleveland tried to soothe African Americans' fears of a Democratic president. He told them that he would ensure that all former slaves were treated the same as whites, as guaranteed by law. Frederick Douglass, a famous former slave and abolitionist (slavery opponent), praised Cleveland's words. The two men considered themselves friends.

Cleveland did give government jobs to blacks. But he granted no special favors to African Americans or any other group. He fully agreed with the ideas of Booker T. Washington. Washington was an African American who gave speeches about the importance of hard work and technical training for blacks. He believed that his people should fight for fair treatment, but he warned them to do so quietly. In Alabama he founded the Tuskegee Institute, a technical training school for African Americans. Some black citizens felt that Washington's approach was too timid. They thought it was important to speak out against racial

——————————— ✧
Booker T. Washington advised African Americans not to bring down the wrath of racists by loud protests. The late 1880s was a time of increased violence against blacks, and opinions differed greatly on how to respond.

discrimination, whether or not that made some whites unhappy. But Washington's ideas fit perfectly with Cleveland's.

In the fall of 1887, the Clevelands took a train trip through the South and to Saint Louis, Missouri. It was the president's first time west of the Mississippi River. Everywhere he went, audiences gave him a hearty welcome.

At a public gathering in Saint Paul, Minnesota, Cleveland broke a record—he shook more hands at a single event than any other president ever had. He shook hands with six thousand people, at a rate of forty-seven shakes a minute! Abraham Lincoln had held the record before him.

✧ ————————————

A souvenir of Cleveland's stop in Saint Louis, Missouri, in October 1887

THE CHINESE EXCLUSION ACTS

Following the Civil War, the number of immigrants to the United States rose sharply. Some Americans did not welcome the newcomers. They formed groups that spoke out against immigrants and tried to get laws passed to stop or slow immigration. Many people blamed immigrants for flooding the job market with too many workers. With so much labor available, employers were less willing to treat their workers well. If a worker quit a job because of unfair treatment, three others were waiting in line to take the job.

For his time, Cleveland was accepting of immigrants. But he held them to the same standards as he did African Americans and Native Americans. He urged immigrants to try to act, talk, and look like those who were born in the United States. They should be proud to become citizens.

In the 1800s, Chinese immigrants worked in mining and railroad construction. For little money, they did the most dangerous and dirtiest jobs.

European American residents of Denver, Colorado, attack Chinese workers in 1880. Cleveland did not support this kind of violence.

✧ ————————————

Many Americans, especially in the West, resented Chinese immigrants in particular for increasing the workforce. Cleveland defended Chinese workers' right to protection under the law. But he didn't feel they would ever really fit in. They lived in their own neighborhoods, called Chinatowns. Many saw no reason to speak English. And many Chinese, who wore their hair in long braids, refused to cut their hair to look like other Americans. They wore Chinese clothes and practiced Chinese customs.

In 1888 Cleveland signed one of a series of laws intended to stop Chinese people from coming into the United States.

Known as the Chinese Exclusion Acts, they were the only laws in U.S. history that turned people away because of their race.

Cleveland explained that the "experiment of blending the social habits and [other differences] of the Chinese laboring classes with those of. . . the people of the United States has proved. . . to be in every sense unwise. . . and [hurtful] to both nations." As he saw it, Chinese immigrants just weren't willing to blend in with other Americans. More important, many planned to go back to China after they had saved enough money. They had no intention of becoming citizens.

For Cleveland the important issue was not a person's race or background. It was his or her willingness to fit into U.S. society. In fact, when Congress tried to pass a law to keep out immigrants who could not read English, he vetoed it. He said that the ability to read or write did not predict people's ability to become good citizens. If they were willing to learn, he was willing to let them enter the country.

CHAPTER SEVEN

YOU WIN SOME, YOU LOSE SOME

It was mainly because the other party had the most votes.

—Grover Cleveland's response, when asked why he lost the presidency to Benjamin Harrison in the 1888 election

Cleveland had won the hearts of the people he met on his 1887 trip through the South. But by 1888, the year he was up for reelection, he had angered many groups. Soldiers didn't like Cleveland because he had stopped so many pensions. Farmers didn't like him because they wanted higher tariffs. Some Democrats didn't want Cleveland to have another term in office because he hadn't given jobs to their friends.

But Democratic Party members did agree on one thing: they didn't have a better candidate than Cleveland for the job. Even many Republicans felt that Cleveland was a good president.

Because Cleveland's foes had no strong criticisms of his performance in office, once again they resorted to personal attacks. The main accusation was that Cleveland beat his wife. Stories circulated that the president had thrown Frances out of the White House while he was dead drunk. In a letter to a friend, the president wrote, "I am sure of one thing. I have in [Frances] something better than the presidency for life—though the Republican parties and the papers do say I beat and abuse her."

Frances finally put a stop to the false stories. She responded to a letter from a woman who had told her that her local clergyman had spoken of the president's bad treatment of his wife. Frances wrote, "I can only say that [the clergyman] speaks wicked and heartless lies. [There is] no. . . [husband] as kind, attentive, considerate, and affectionate as mine." The Republican press denied that it was the source of the rumors. Many people thought that Cleveland's longtime enemies at Tammany Hall had made up the stories.

——————— ✧
In Cleveland's reelection campaign in 1888, he continued to stick to issues. This campaign poster from 1888 states Cleveland's opinion about tariffs.

THE 1888 ELECTION

The Republican presidential candidate was Benjamin Harrison, an Indiana senator who was the grandson of the country's ninth president, William Henry Harrison. The Republicans knew that the senator wasn't the best man for the job. Many people did not like Harrison. He had a habit of taking long pauses when someone asked him a question. People said that shaking his hand was like grasping a wet petunia. But Harrison was a big fan of higher tariffs. And tariffs were the most important issue in this election.

Harrison's handshake may have been limp, but his campaign fundraisers were not. They raised more than three million dollars from business leaders for his campaign. Some historians argue that this was the beginning of the modern practice of raising huge campaign funds to increase the chances of winning the election.

Cleveland's campaign staff, in contrast, did not work very hard to win. They decided to sit back and wait for the Republicans to make a mistake that would keep Harrison from winning.

Cleveland had several things working against him in the election. He had made enemies during his first four years in office. Instead of running hard for reelection, he spent his energy on his job as president. He also had a weak running mate. The Democrats chose Governor Allen Thurman of Ohio to run as Cleveland's vice-presidential candidate. (Vice President Hendricks had died in his first year in office, and the job had gone unfilled.) Thurman called for raising tariffs, while Cleveland wanted to lower them. The governor was also in poor health.

After the voting took place on November 6, 1888, Cleveland won the popular vote. He received about 100,000 more votes from the people than Harrison. But Cleveland lost the electoral vote 168 to 233, making Harrison the next president.

POPULAR AND ELECTORAL VOTES

U.S. citizens do not vote directly for the president. When they go to the polls in their home state, they vote for a group of officials called electors. The electors promise to vote for certain candidates, although the presidential candidate who wins a majority of the state's popular votes (votes from citizens) wins all the state's electoral votes.

All the electors' votes together are called the electoral vote. The people's votes are called the popular vote. Both of these votes are counted. But the electoral vote decides who becomes president. The nation's founding fathers chose this system to foster a calm decision-making process and support states' rights.

Each state has the same number of electors as it has members of Congress. For example, California has fifty-five members of Congress, so it has fifty-five electors. Wyoming has only three Congressional seats, so it has just three electors. The fifty states and the District of Columbia have a total of 538 electors and 538 electoral votes. To win, a candidate needs 270 electoral votes.

Most of the time, the president wins both the electoral and popular votes. But this didn't happen in 1824, 1876, 1888, and 2000. In these election years, the president lost the popular vote but won the electoral vote, and thus the presidency.

Cleveland was surprised when he lost. But he wasn't unhappy. He looked forward to spending time with his wife away from the White House. He and Frances moved to a four-story home on Madison Avenue in New York City. Cleveland went back to the practice of law.

THE REPUBLICAN PLAN

The Republicans had not only put Harrison in the White House, but they also won more seats in Congress than the Democrats. From New York, Cleveland kept a close watch on what was going on in Washington. He was curious to see what a Republican administration backed by a Republican Congress would do. One of the first things the new president did was raise tariffs. Tariffs on foreign goods brought into the United States were the highest they'd ever been. Next, Congress passed the Sherman Silver Purchase Act of 1890. This law forced the government to buy silver to use in coins. The act also created a steady demand for silver, making it more valuable.

Harrison liked Cleveland's changes to the spoils system and tried to continue them. But Congress quickly stopped that and went back to the old system. Thousands of Democrats lost their jobs. The government began granting more veterans' pensions again. Little by little, the Republican president and lawmakers undid nearly everything Cleveland had achieved.

In response to the higher tariffs, the price of U.S.-made goods went up. U.S. producers knew that they could safely raise prices. Foreign producers, paying more to export their goods to the United States, had to raise their prices too. As prices of all products went up, Americans bought fewer things. The economy slipped.

The value of silver went up at first. But as more silver was mined and sold, supply exceeded demand—more silver was available than buyers for it—and the price fell. Because of the Sherman Silver Act, the government owned a lot of silver. The drop in the value of silver caused a drop in the value of the U.S. dollar. As the dollar sank in value, manufacturers and farmers got more dollars for their products. But they needed more dollars to pay for the materials to make those products.

While the value of silver went down, the value of gold went up. This caused a rush to trade in silver dollars for gold. The U.S. Treasury's gold supply dropped. By 1891 the country was in big trouble, heading for financial disaster.

——————— ✧

The value of silver dropped during Harrison's term in office (1889–1893). Many people traded their silver dollars for gold. This kept bank and U.S. Treasury employees busy weighing and counting coins.

Congress had passed the Sherman Anti-Trust Act in 1890. This law, like the Interstate Commerce Act, was supposed to stop individuals or businesses from gaining control over particular industries, such as oil or steel. The businesses formed illegal groups called trusts. Working together, they controlled prices and drove smaller companies out of business.

ELECTION OF 1892

For a while, Cleveland was content to watch politics from a distance. He enjoyed the time he had to take walks, go on vacations to a summer house in Massachusetts, and have quiet dinners with Frances. In October 1891, Frances gave birth to the Clevelands' first child, Ruth.

The Clevelands named their first child Ruth. She was born in 1891.

Cleveland, fifty-four years old, was very happy. He wrote to a friend that "he had entered the real world."

Still, as the U.S. economy grew weaker, Cleveland became concerned about many of the decisions and actions of the Harrison administration. He began to think of running for president again to keep the country from disaster.

The Democrats were split over the sound money policy that Cleveland favored. Some liked his ideas. Some didn't. They chose him as their presidential candidate anyway in 1892. Cleveland spoke out against the Sherman Silver Act and the rise in tariffs. To some Democrats, he sounded like he was worried only about the country's money. He didn't seem concerned about farmers or workers.

Still, most Americans wanted Cleveland back in the White House. In the election of 1892, Cleveland easily won. Voters hoped that he would be able to save them from ruin.

*This souvenir postcard celebrates
the Clevelands' return to the White House
in 1894.*

CHAPTER EIGHT

OLD BATTLES AND NEW TRENDS

I am not the sort of man people want to hear
these days. My beliefs and opinions are
unsuited for the times.
—Grover Cleveland, 1899

Cleveland took his second presidential oath on March 4, 1893. He is the only U.S. president ever to serve two terms that were not in a row. That year, the country was sliding into a very deep depression, a time of slowed economic activity. In fact, it was the worst economic trouble in U.S. history. Within a year, fifteen thousand companies went out of business and five hundred banks failed. Almost 30 percent of U.S. railroads went broke. This ruined many steel producers, who relied on the railroads to transport steel.

As soon as Cleveland got back in the White House, he started trying to improve the country's economy. At the same time, he was busy hiring and firing people again, which took up a lot of time.

SECRET SURGERY

That summer, Cleveland was facing a serious health problem. Doctors had found a spot in his mouth that proved to be cancer. A longtime cigar smoker, Cleveland needed to act fast. He knew that reports of his cancer could make people in the financial business nervous about the future of the nation and send the stock market into a tailspin. If news that he was sick got out, it might make the country's money problems worse.

The president agreed to surgery but only if it could be done in secret. He talked his doctors into operating aboard a yacht owned by a friend. As the boat made its way up New York City's East River, the medical team successfully removed the tumor from Cleveland's mouth. They also had to remove part of his upper jaw. A few weeks later, doctors fitted him with a rubber plug to fill the hole. Then he went about his business as usual. People suspected that he was in poor health, but the full story didn't leak out.

The Clevelands enjoyed one bright spot in 1893. Their second child, Esther, was born in September.

HARD TIMES

By 1894 the depression had worsened. One-third of all U.S. factory workers had lost their jobs. Every day more people were joining the ranks of the unemployed. The silver mines in the West were boarded up. The stock market went into a free fall.

Cleveland asked Congress to get rid of the Sherman Silver Act. The Republicans and Democrats fought over the issue.

A Private Matter

Cleveland was carrying on a presidential tradition when he kept his cancer a secret from the public. When George Washington turned a pale shade of green and went to bed with a high fever in 1789, his staff concluded that he had the flu. But Thomas Jefferson warned them not to tell anyone. He feared that people might panic if they knew their president was ill. Jefferson himself was bedridden at the time with one of his chronic migraine headaches.

During the Civil War, Abraham Lincoln came down with what was probably smallpox. "A mild case of varioloid [chicken pox]," his aides told the public. "Complete recovery expected!" they quickly added.

In 1882 Chester Arthur told the press that he was definitely not suffering from Bright's disease, a deadly kidney condition. Four years later, Arthur died from a group of ailments, including kidney failure.

When President Woodrow Wilson had a near-fatal stroke in 1919, his wife and his doctor told reporters that the president was doing great—he was walking well and was the picture of health. Wilson, in fact, lay in his bed for nearly two months, barely conscious. His wife took up the slack, and the government carried on without Wilson's active participation.

Near the end of World War II (1939–1945), Franklin Delano Roosevelt's doctors kept his fatal heart condition a secret not only to the press but also from the president himself. The truth about John Kennedy's heavy medication for Addison's disease, a hormonal problem, did not come out for decades. The president, who served from 1960 to 1963, seemed to have a constant, healthy-looking tan, which was actually a discoloring of his skin caused by the disease.

Cleveland (second from left) faced a tough second term. His cabinet
members included Daniel Scott Lamont, War Secretary (left), *and (to*
the right of Cleveland, left to right) *John Griffin Carlisle, Treasury;*
Richard Olney, attorney general; Walter Quintin Gresham, State; Julius
Sterling Morton, Agriculture; Hoke Smith, Interior; Wilson Shannon
Bissell, postmaster-general; Hilary Abner Herbert, Navy.

In the end, legislators decided to give the president what
he wanted. The silver act was killed. But the split over the
issue in the Democratic Party deepened as the economy got
worse.

Cleveland was popular with the public when he began his
second term, but this public approval did not last long.
Farmers in the South and the West once again accused him
of pushing the interests of big business. When Cleveland
tried to boost the U.S. Treasury's shrinking gold reserves,
people charged him with making profits for the wealthy.
They didn't like the deal he made with financial tycoon J. P.

Morgan. Morgan traded the government sixty million dollars in gold for some very profitable government investments.

Cleveland continued to fight for lower tariffs in his second term. Cleveland lost his fight when Senate Democrats, bowing to pressure from farmers, manufacturers, and silver producers, joined forces with the Republicans. Together they pushed the Wilson-Gorman Tariff Act through Congress. The first version of the bill lowered tariffs. But after Congress added six hundred amendments (changes) to the act, the final version raised tariffs again. The bill became law in 1894.

PROTEST MARCHES AND WORKERS' STRIKES

The ongoing depression hit farmers and working people hard. They looked to the U.S. government for help. Some people who were tired of being poor and jobless gathered together to march in protest to Washington, D.C. They felt that the government was not doing enough to aid its people.

The marchers were led by an Ohio farmer named Jacob Coxey. Coxey had a plan. He proposed that the U.S.

────────── ✧

Coxey's followers were known as Coxey's Army. In 1898 many walked more than 350 miles from Ohio to Washington, D.C., to protest joblessness.

government could hire the men who had lost their jobs and put them to work to repair and improve the country's roads, bridges, and dams.

Coxey arrived in Washington on May 1, 1894. He brought with him his infant son, named Legal Tender. His band of followers was known as Coxey's Army. Police quickly arrested Coxey for being on the Capitol lawn. They tossed him in jail, where he stayed for nearly three weeks.

As the depression continued, more workers protested. Labor unions took action, including a major railroad strike in May 1894. George Pullman, owner of the Pullman Palace Car Company in Chicago, had earned a fortune by making train travel much more comfortable. He built luxury trains that featured dining cars and the cozy Pullman sleeping car. While Pullman raked in the money, his workers lived in poverty. Not only did he pay them low wages but he also required them to rent their homes from him. Workers were also told to shop only at stores owned by the company. Pullman priced the goods at his stores as high as possible.

In the spring of 1894, Pullman cut worker pay by 25 percent. He claimed that the wage cut was necessary because of the economic depression. He did not lower the cost of rent or anything else to make up for the cut in pay. In response, several thousand Pullman workers went on strike. Pullman fired them all. Then he closed down the factory.

The Pullman workers' union, the American Railway Union, ordered all 150,000 members to act. They would no longer run any train that included Pullman cars. The strike stopped rail service throughout much of the United States.

Railroad owners wanted the U.S. government to force the strikers back to work. To make their point, the railroad companies connected Pullman cars to the trains that carried the U.S. mail. The companies knew that this would force the government to get involved, since mail delivery was so important. Attorney General Richard Olney advised President Cleveland to send out U.S. troops to break the strike. Cleveland was concerned about the workers and their problems, but he knew that he had to keep the mail going. He sent U.S. Army soldiers to confront the strikers in early July. "If it takes the entire army and navy of the United States to deliver a post card in Chicago," he reportedly thundered, "that card will be delivered."

Partially shielded by derailed railroad cars, Illinois National Guardsmen take aim at Pullman strikers on July 7, 1894.

The strikers fought back with rocks and sticks, and a mob attacked the soldiers. Riots broke out in Chicago. After days of violence, several people were dead and hundreds injured. The rioting and striking finally ended on July 8, but the event left many Americans angry at Cleveland and his administration.

FALLING OUT OF FAVOR

As early as the 1894 congressional election, voters showed their anger by going to the polls. They blamed Cleveland for the country's problems. The public had sent Cleveland back to the White House to save the country, and he had failed. In the election that fall, every region, except the Deep South, voted against the Democratic candidates. This put Congress back in the hands of the Republicans.

The next year, Cleveland's popularity took another dive.

Attorney General Richard Olney
——————— ✧ ———————

By 1895 several big U.S. sugar companies had joined together to fix prices and drive out smaller companies. The Sherman Anti-Trust Act made this illegal. Farmers and small-business owners pushed Attorney General Olney into filing a suit against the sugar monopoly. Olney faced a tough choice. Should he please the farmers and small businessmen—or the big sugar companies? He came down in the middle. He filed the suit, but he argued it so poorly that the court quickly threw it out.

Farmers and small business owners were angry. They felt that Olney had lost the case on purpose. When Cleveland defended Olney, matters got worse. Although he had spoken many times about the greed of big business, Cleveland seemed to be supporting the rich. Public opinion and the Democrats turned against him. He felt betrayed not only by the voters but also by his own political party.

1895 had been a difficult year for the president, but in July Frances Cleveland gave birth to a third child, Marion.

——————————— ✧ ———————————

A busier mother than ever during Cleveland's second term in office (1893–1897), Frances (center) found time to pose for this photograph with the wives of Cleveland's cabinet members.

Cleveland's three young daughters brought laughter and joy to the White House.

FOREIGN POLICY

At the end of his presidency, Benjamin Harrison had asked Congress to approve a treaty that let the United States take over the Hawaiian Islands. At the time, Hawaii was not part of the United States, though it had strong economic ties to the country. Americans with business interests in the islands had pressured Harrison to get the treaty made into law. When Cleveland took office, however, he withdrew the treaty before Congress could pass it. He believed that the Hawaiian people had the right to govern themselves under their queen, Liliuokalani. Furthermore, Cleveland felt that the United States would be misusing its power by taking over Hawaii.

Soon after the Hawaii issue, Cleveland showed that he was willing to defend U.S. interests when he felt he was in the right. In 1895 Great Britain tried to add part of Venezuela to its South American colony, British Guiana. Cleveland sharply reminded British leaders of the Monroe Doctrine. Written in 1823, the doctrine forbade world powers from claiming any more territory in the Western Hemisphere. The doctrine said that the United States would protect other countries from such land-grabbing. The British knew Cleveland meant business and backed off.

In the 1890s, U.S. farmers and business leaders pushed harder to increase U.S. trade with foreign countries. Some people accused Cleveland of not using foreign markets to boost U.S. trade. They figured that the United States could follow the lead of powers like Spain and Britain and take over weaker countries as colonies. This would ensure markets for U.S. goods. Cleveland was against it.

He also opposed a movement to help the Spanish colony of Cuba free itself from Spanish control. When Cubans rose up against Spain in 1895, some Americans favored stepping in to help. Cleveland believed that the United States could use diplomacy to persuade the Spanish into giving Cuba its independence. On December 7, 1896, Cleveland sent his last message to Congress. In it he declared that Americans should do what was right in Cuba, not what was within their power.

Cleveland and his son Richard (born in 1897) pause for a photograph outside of Westland, their home in Princeton, New Jersey.

CHAPTER NINE

RETIREMENT

I don't know in the shuffle what will become
of me and my poor old battered name.
—Grover Cleveland, in a letter to a friend, 1896

Well before the elections of 1896, Cleveland knew that it was time to retire. He'd had a good run—thirty years in public office. At age fifty-nine, he was slowing down. He had lost as much as sixty pounds following his cancer surgery three years earlier. But probably more important, the public had turned against him. Everyone seemed to blame him for the country's problems. Both Democrats and Republicans opposed him. Many Americans felt that he was out of touch with working people.

Cleveland still believed that gold was the safest basis for U.S. currency. Big business, bankers, and investors who put their money in the stock market agreed with him. Poorer folks were convinced that Cleveland's monetary policies benefited only the wealthy. Organized labor hadn't

Cleveland (right) *stands by as Chief Justice Melville Weston Fuller* (left) *administers the oath of office to Cleveland's successor, William McKinley.*

✧ ————————

forgotten that the president had used U.S. troops against the unions. Many veterans were still unhappy about his stand on Civil War pensions. Farmers had opposed Cleveland's lower tariffs for a long time. His decisions on foreign policy also ran against public opinion.

The Democratic Party was divided again. In 1895 the Democrats had chosen former congressman William Jennings Bryan to run as their presidential candidate in 1896. Bryan favored the "bimetallic standard," the idea of basing the U.S. economy on both silver and gold.

Cleveland did not want to serve a third term. (Until 1951 presidents could serve as many terms as they were elected to.) His supporters in the party held their own convention and chose him anyway. He turned them down. Bryan went on to challenge William McKinley, the Republican candidate. Bryan and the silver interests were defeated. Some people saw McKinley's election as a victory for Cleveland, since McKinley supported Cleveland's ideas about the gold standard.

THE PRINCETON YEARS

The Clevelands retired to Princeton, New Jersey, in 1897. That year Frances gave birth to their fourth child. They named this first son Richard Folsom.

Even after leaving the White House, Cleveland remained a busy man. He taught at Princeton University and gave business advice to several large companies. Many organizations asked him to speak at their meetings and events. He also wrote articles for magazines, such as the *Atlantic* and *Ladies' Home Journal.* For gentlemen's magazines, he wrote about hunting and fishing.

Cleveland spent a lot of time in his library at Princeton.

On August 12, 1898, a crowd watches the U.S. flag go up over Iolani Palace, the former Hawaiian royal residence in Honolulu, Hawaii. The event marked the U.S. takeover of Hawaii.
✧ ———————

Cleveland continued to keep up with politics. In 1898, with McKinley's approval, Congress went ahead and passed the treaty to take over the Hawaiian Islands. Cleveland was not pleased with this show of U.S. imperialism (the practice of taking over other governments for gain). He joined the Anti-Imperialist League, a group that tried to stop the United States' growing hunger for world power.

While still president, Cleveland had tried to avoid a conflict with Spain over the issue of Cuba's independence. But he only delayed the fight. When a U.S. ship, the *Maine*, blew up in a Cuban harbor in February 1898, Americans blamed the Spanish. On April 25, 1898, the United States declared war on Spain. The Spanish-American War lasted only a few months, with a quick U.S. victory. In the treaty that ended the war, the United States gained control of the

Spanish colonies Guam, Puerto Rico, and the Philippine Islands. In 1900 the United States also made the Hawaiian Islands an official territory.

When Cleveland left office in 1897, he felt that his own party had mistreated him and that the public hated him. But in the spring of 1903, the people of Saint Louis, Missouri, gave him a pleasant surprise. They asked him to attend their Louisiana Purchase Exposition, a huge celebration honoring the Louisiana Purchase, the largest land deal the United States ever made. When Cleveland got up to speak, the crowd welcomed him warmly. People clapped and cheered so loudly that Cleveland knew they no longer blamed him for their difficulties.

————————— ✧
A crowd gathers for opening day speeches and performances at the 1903 Louisiana Purchase Exposition in Saint Louis, Missouri. Cleveland was one of the speakers during the exposition.

In July 1903, Frances gave birth to the Clevelands' fifth child, a boy named Francis. Cleveland, at the age of sixty-six, was filled with joy. But just six months later, on January 7, 1904, the Clevelands faced tragedy. They lost their twelve-year-old daughter, Ruth, to a common childhood disease, diphtheria. The next day, Cleveland made a sad entry in his diary: "January 8. We buried our daughter, Ruth, this morning." His hand shook so badly that the writing could hardly be read. In the days that followed, Cleveland was in such despair that he questioned his belief in an afterlife. On January 11, he wrote in his diary, "It seems to me I mourn our darling Ruth's death more and more. So much of the time I can only think of her as dead, not joyfully living in Heaven."

By the end of April 1904, Cleveland had accepted Ruth's death and believed that she was beyond harm. He wrote to his sister Mary, "[I] have not a shadow of a doubt that all is well with the child."

Grover Cleveland in 1908
——————— ✧ ———————

THE SUM OF A MAN

In 1904 Cleveland published a book titled *Presidential Problems* about his years in office. The public eagerly read it. On Cleveland's sixty-ninth birthday, the U.S. flag flew all over New York in respect for the former president. Mark Twain compared him to George Washington and said he was a man of honesty and courage.

Cleveland lived seventy-one years. When he died of heart failure on June 24, 1908, his family and the nation grieved for him.

After Cleveland's death, many newspapers printed articles about his years in office. The first reviews of his two terms as president were warm. Written by friends and fellow Democrats, the articles praised his strength of character and sense of purpose. In the first half of the twentieth century, historians praised his honesty and clear thinking.

But later scholars criticized Cleveland for his nineteenth-century views about racial issues and women's rights. For instance, some historians wondered why Cleveland never spoke out against the Jim Crow laws in the South. These laws made it legal to discriminate against African Americans. Others questioned his support of the Chinese Exclusion Acts, laws that kept Chinese people from settling in the United States just because of their race. And some asked why he hadn't worked for women's voting rights (American women were not able to vote until 1920).

Most modern historians see Cleveland as a nearly great president. Unlike Abraham Lincoln or Franklin Delano Roosevelt, Grover Cleveland didn't change the course of U.S. history in a truly important way. He is remembered, instead, because he stayed true to his own word and to the words of the Constitution. He set an example of honesty and courage in a time of public dishonesty and weakness. Most important, he renewed the American people's faith in government, at least for a while. Cleveland's dying words were, "I have tried so hard to do right." He was, by habit, speaking the truth.

TIMELINE

1837   Stephen Grover Cleveland is born March 18 in Caldwell, New Jersey. The United States is in a financial crisis.

1841   The Cleveland family moves to Fayetteville, New York.

1853   Cleveland's father, Richard Falley Cleveland, dies. Grover takes a job at the New York Institution for the Blind.

1854   The Kansas-Nebraska Act causes a violent showdown between activists on both sides of the slavery issue.

1855   With the help of an uncle, Cleveland begins to study law in Buffalo, New York.

1859   Cleveland is admitted to the New York State Bar at the age of twenty-two and begins work as a lawyer.

1861–1865   The American Civil War rages over the issues of slavery and preserving the Union.

1862   Cleveland is elected as a Democratic ward supervisor in Buffalo. Later that year, he becomes assistant district attorney for Erie County, New York.

1863   The Union drafts Cleveland into its army, but he pays someone else to serve in his place.

1870   Cleveland is elected sheriff of Erie County for a three-year term.

1874   Cleveland returns to the practice of law, forming a company with Oscar Folsom. Oscar Folsom Cleveland, rumored to be Cleveland's son with Maria Halpin, is born.

1881   Cleveland is elected mayor of Buffalo.

1882   Cleveland's mother, Ann, dies in July. In November Cleveland is elected governor of New York.

1884   Cleveland wins the election to become president of the United States.

1885   On Cleveland's first day in office, more than fifty thousand miners are on strike.

1886   Railroad workers across the country go on strike, stopping all trains. Some worker protests turn violent, including the Haymarket Riot in Chicago. Cleveland uses U.S. troops against the strikers. On June 2, Cleveland marries Frances Folsom.

1887   Cleveland signs the Interstate Commerce Act, which makes it illegal for railroad owners to form monopolies and fix their prices. He also approves the Dawes Act, which gives U.S. citizenship and private ownership of a piece of land to every Native American.

1888   In October Cleveland signs an act meant to keep Chinese people from immigrating to the United States. In November he wins the popular vote for president but loses the electoral vote. Benjamin Harrison is elected.

1892   The Democrats choose Cleveland to run for president again. Cleveland easily beats Harrison and becomes the twenty-fourth president.

1893   Cleveland blocks a treaty allowing the United States to take over Hawaii. On May 4, the stock market crashes. In June Cleveland has cancer surgery in secret.

1894   Cleveland tries to build up U.S. Treasury gold reserves by selling government bonds to J. P. Morgan. He also gets Congress to temporarily lower tariffs, hoping this will help the economy. The president sends U.S. troops to break a rail workers' strike in Chicago.

1896   Cleveland refuses to run for a third term. The Democratic candidate, William Jennings Bryan, loses the election to Republican William McKinley.

1897   The Clevelands retire to Princeton, New Jersey.

1898   The Spanish-American War lasts from April until August. Spain loses and the United States gains control of the Philippines, Guam, and Puerto Rico.

1908   Cleveland dies in Princeton, New Jersey, on June 24 at age seventy-one.

SOURCE NOTES

7   Alyn Brodsky, *Grover Cleveland: A Study in Character* (New York: St. Martin's Press, 2000), 52.

8   H. Paul Jeffers, *An Honest President: The Life and Presidencies of Grover Cleveland* (New York: William Morrow, 2000), 368.

9   Henry F. Graff, *Grover Cleveland* (New York: Henry Holt, 2002), 7.

11 Robert McNutt McElroy, *Grover Cleveland: The Man and the Statesman*, vol. 1 (New York: Harper & Brothers, 1923), 35.

20 William C. Hudson, *Random Recollections of an Old Political Reporter* (New York: Cupples & Leon, 1911), 179–80.

25 Ibid.

27 Allan Nevins, ed., *The Letters of Grover Cleveland: 1850–1908* (New York: Da Capo Press, 1970), 17–18.

30 Ibid., 35.

34 Brodsky, *Grover Cleveland*, 89.

36 Marvin Rosenberg and Dorothy Rosenberg, "The Dirtiest Election," *American Heritage*, August 1962, 4.

36 Ibid.

36 Ibid.

38 Gail Collins, *Scorpion Tongues: Gossip, Celebrity, and American Politics* (New York: William Morrow, 1998), 30.

38 Ibid.

39 Brodsky, *Grover Cleveland*, 95.

41 Hudson, *Random Recollections of an Old Political Reporter*, 209.

41 Paul Boller, *Presidential Anecdotes* (New York: Oxford University Press, 2001), 179.

43 Nevins, *The Letters of Grover Cleveland*, 46.

46 Ibid., 103.

46 Ibid., 105.

51 Brodsky, *Grover Cleveland*, 141.

56 Ibid., 164.

56 Nevins, *The Letters of Grover Cleveland*, 103.

56 Ibid., 106.

58 Grover Cleveland, "Woman's Mission and Women's Clubs," *Ladies Home Journal*, May 1905.

65 George F. Parker, *The Writings and Speeches of Grover Cleveland* (New York: Cassell Publishing, 1970), 118.

68 "Sitting Bull," *Power Source*, N.d., http://www.powersource .com/gallery/people/sittbull.html (January 28, 2005).

69 Nevins, *The Letters of Grover Cleveland*, 180.

75 Brodsky, *Grover Cleveland*, 456.

76 McElroy, *Grover Cleveland*, 307.

77 Nevins, *The Letters of Grover Cleveland*, 183–4.

77 McElroy, *Grover Cleveland*, 286.

83 Nevins, *The Letters of Grover Cleveland*, 269.

85 Ibid., 515.

87 Dr. Zebra (John Sotos, M.D.), "The Medical History of American Presidents," *Dr. Zebra*, n.d., http://www.doctorzebra .com/prez/index.htm (January 29, 2005).

91 "Grover Cleveland," *The White House*, n.d., http://www.white-house.gov/history/presidents/ gc2224.html (October 18, 2004).

97 Nevins, *The Letters of Grover Cleveland*, 462.

102 Brodsky, *Grover Cleveland*, 427.

102 Nevins, *The Letters of Grover Cleveland*, 741.

102 Ibid.

103 Graff, *Grover Cleveland*, 135.

SELECTED BIBLIOGRAPHY

Boller, Paul. *Presidential Anecdotes*. New York: Oxford University Press, 2001.

Brodsky, Alyn. *Grover Cleveland: A Study in Character*. New York: St. Martin's Press, 2000.

Chicago Public Library. *Chicago Historical Information: The Pullman Strike*. N.d. http://www.chipublib.org/004chicago/disasters/pullman_strike.html (January 27, 2005).

Collins, Gail. *Scorpion Tongues: Gossip, Celebrity, and American Politics*. New York: William Morrow, 1998.

Graff, Henry F. *Grover Cleveland*. New York: Henry Holt, 2002.

Homberger, Eric. *The Historical Atlas of New York City*. New York: Henry Holt, 1998.

Hudson, William C. *Random Recollections of an Old Political Reporter*. New York: Cupples & Leon, 1911.

Jeffers, H. Paul. *An Honest President: The Life and Presidencies of Grover Cleveland*. New York: William Morrow, 2000.

McElroy, Robert McNutt. *Grover Cleveland: The Man and the Statesman*. 2 vols. New York: Harper & Brothers, 1923.

Nevins, Allan, ed. *The Letters of Grover Cleveland 1850–1908*. New York: Da Capo Press, 1970.

Parker, George F. *The Writings and Speeches of Grover Cleveland*. New York: Cassell Publishing, 1970.

Public Broadcasting System. "Gilded Age." *The American Experience*, N.d. http://www.pbs.org/wgbh/amex/carnegie/gildedage.html (January 27, 2005).

Weisberger, Bernard A. "The Press and the Presidents." *American Heritage*, October 1994, 22.

Welch, Richard E. *The Presidencies of Grover Cleveland*. Lawrence: University Press of Kansas, 1988.

FURTHER READING AND WEBSITES

Adelson, Bruce. *Benjamin Harrison.* Minneapolis: Lerner Publications Company, 2007.

Arnold, by James R.. *The Civil War.* Minneapolis: Lerner Publications Company, 2005.

"Biography of Grover Cleveland." *The White House.* http://www.whitehouse.gov/history/presidents The official White House website provides concise biographies of all the presidents.

The Grover Cleveland Birthplace. http://www.westessexguide.com/gcb/index.htm This site describes a collection of Cleveland's personal belongings, including his cradle and his fishing gear, as well as some rare photos of him.

Hess, Stephen, and Sandy Northrop. *Drawn & Quartered: The History of American Political Cartoons.* Montgomery, AL: Elliot & Clark, 1996.

Kendall, Martha E. *Failure Is Impossible! The History of American Women's Rights.* Minneapolis: Twenty-First Century Books, 2001

"Let Your Tragedy Be Enacted Here." *Chicago Historical Society.* http://www.chicagohs.org/dramas/overview/resource.htm This is an excellent history of the Haymarket Riot.

Moore, Jacqueline M. *Booker T. Washington, W.E.B. Du Bois, and the Struggle for Racial Uplift.* Wilmington, DE: Scholarly Resources, 2003.

"Presidential Inaugural Address." *Great Books Online.* http://www.bartleby.com/124/pres37.html This site provides the texts of U.S. presidents' inaugural speeches, including the two delivered by Grover Cleveland.

Rubel, David. *Scholastic Encyclopedia of the Presidents and Their Times.* New York: Scholastic, 1997.

"Sitting Bull." *Powersource.* http:www.powersource.com/gallery/people/sittbull.html A biography of the Sioux leader, including many quotations by him.

INDEX

ABOUT THE AUTHOR

Rita J. Markel's stories and historical articles for children and teens have appeared in magazines and books (some under her pseudonym, Bonnie Brightman). She has written on such topics as rock legend Jimi Hendrix, America's Old West, ancient Rome, the Gee-Bee racing planes, and the U.S. Army Camel Corps. She lives in Boise, Idaho.

———————— ✧ ————————